40 Tips for Holiday Money Saving

JENNIFER VARGAS

Table of Contents

Holiday potlucks are being held.

Invest in LED bulbs.

Save money by making a gift request.

Making a Volunteering Gift.

Create a "No-Gift Christmas".

The National Retail Federation predicted that retail sales will increase by 3.6% to 4% in November and December, reaching $682 billion. And according to a recent GOBankingRates poll, over two-thirds of Americans want to spend at least $100 more on holiday shopping this year than usual.

Spending at the end of the year may break any committed saver's budget between the holiday ham and toys for the kids. Here are 40 strategies for reducing holiday expenditures and relieving financial stress.

Chapter 1

Set Up a Spending Budget

- Knowing how much you can spend beforehand will prevent you from going into debt or otherwise wrecking your money. Natasha Campbell, a personal finance expert, advised making a list of everyone you intend to buy gifts for and deciding how much you are ready to spend on each recipient.

Consider how much you'll have to spend on food, decorations, and entertainment once you've set a reasonable present budget. It will be easier to save money in advance and keep you alert when you're shopping if you know how much your expenses are likely to rise.

Purchase Gifts Little by Little

- In addition to overpaying for some things during the holiday rush, Regina Conway, consumer expert at Slickdeals, noted that doing everything in one day will put more strain on your pocketbook.

Spreading out your purchases across the coming months will allow you to budget well and prevent a credit hangover in January, she advised. Additionally, it will enable you to benefit from the different specials that run during the holiday season.

Establish Reasonable Expectations.

It's okay if your children don't fully comprehend your financial situation as long as you work with them to set reasonable expectations for gifts. Establishing a defined budget for their gifts can help your children create a gift wishlist rather than letting them swoon over every new toy and gadget that's released this holiday season.

Shopping for loved ones will be less stressful if you know your children won't be expecting the newest video games, a pony, or other exorbitantly priced presents. Additionally, it helps your children realize that the holidays aren't only about acquiring the sexiest gifts they can show off at school.

Knowing when to shop

- Every year, retailers work harder to entice customers into their stores earlier and earlier, but it doesn't guarantee that they will find the best prices, according to managing editor of Ben's Bargains Kristin Cook.

For instance, she noted that December is frequently when video game consoles and toys have the cheapest discounts.

To assist you in determining when and where the best prices are, websites like BFAds produce thorough buying guides. You can decide wisely whether to buy now or wait until Black Friday by looking at the greatest current bargains alongside forthcoming Black Friday specials on FatWallet.

Brent Shelton, an online shopping specialist with BFAds, stated that being aware of when items go on sale can help you be one of the fortunate ones to snag those constrained, time-sensitive discounts.

Shop early in November.

- For the finest deals of the year, you don't have to leave your Thanksgiving dinner to brave the Black Friday crowds.

Starting in early November, a number of product categories, including electronics and home appliances, will be reduced to Black Friday pricing, according to Cook. Stores like Amazon, Best Buy,

Target, and Walmart may be offering these early holiday bargains.

Establish Deal Alerts

- To keep up with sales and ensure you don't miss out, Shelton advised signing up for deal alerts.

For instance, you will be notified when price reductions are posted in the Fatwallet "Hot Deals" forum by knowledgeable deal hunters. While Slickdeals will notify you whenever a deal is listed that matches the keywords or products you chose.

Chapter 2

The night before Thanksgiving, do your online shopping.

- According to Cook, the best online Thanksgiving offers will begin to go up on Wednesday night.

This includes both announced and unadvertised deals. In truth, many establishments advertise opening at midnight but will informally open an hour sooner to get an advantage over rivals.

Watch merchant websites as bargains go live to catch the greatest offers before inventory runs out. Cook noted that some of the finest offers sold out in an hour, but the majority only lasted a few hours.

Although shops may purposefully plan sales of various goods during Thanksgiving, staying up late the night before Thanksgiving will pay off handsomely, she added.

Get Black Friday Deals

- Following Black Friday Doorbuster prices can be obtained without waiting in line outside of a business at the crack of dawn.

According to Kyle James, the creator of the coupon and deal website Rather-Be-Shopping, you can find numerous things at a discount on eBay a day or two after Black Friday. Black Friday is a popular time for people to buy things and then resell them online for a modest profit.

In order to avoid paying far more than if you had waited in line for hours, he advised checking eBay over the Black Friday weekend.

Make Old Gadgets Into Holiday Cash.

- You may simply transform unused technology, such as cell phones, tablets, PCs, and video gaming consoles, into cash for the holidays.

On websites like Gazelle, NextWorth, and uSell, you may sell any unwanted or damaged devices. Alternatively, you may exchange them for gift cards at stores like Best Buy, Target, and Walmart, according to consumer expert Andrea Woroch. In actuality, your home is full of hidden revenue opportunities that will materialize during the holiday season.

Even leftover ink cartridges can be turned into cash for holiday gifts. If you recycle up to 10 cartridges per month, Staples will give you $2 in rewards, she added.

Purchase pre-owned and refurbished electronics.

- For many holiday consumers, the expense of the newest technology, such as the recently announced iPhone 13, is exorbitant.

Consider purchasing refurbished or old equipment from stores rather than the newest technology. You can save hundreds of dollars by purchasing an earlier model, even modestly.

Purchasing used equipment is what Brian Kramer, a former Gazelle director of communications, advises. Seventy percent of 750 Gazelle customers surveyed felt that the expensive cost of a new iPhone or iPad prevented them from purchasing it as a present, he said, adding that many consumers can find smartphones for up to 40% less than the price of a new item.

The phrase "Stock Up on Discounted Gift Cards"

- When making Christmas shopping, you can save money by purchasing cheap gift cards from websites like CardCash, GiftCards, and Raise.

Conway said that you can use a discounted gift card as money when you shop in addition to giving it as a present. A excellent way to save money when buying online is to use discounted gift cards as cash.

Chapter 3

Buy Unwanted Gift Cards

- You can sell unopened gift cards from last Christmas online for 80% to 90% of their value, according to Phillip Christenson, a financial counselor for Phillip James Financial.

Sites like Cardpool and Giftcard Zen let you sell your cards for cash.

Don't get the upsell

Don't spend more than is necessary. Avoid buying an extended warranty, or at the very least, get a less expensive warranty from a protection plan provider like SquareTrade, advised Shelton.

Avoid shipping costs.

- When it comes to internet buyers saving money during Christmas, don't look much further than delivery costs.

Online shopping makes it simple to compare prices and avoid lines, but shipping costs might completely eat up any savings.

Woroch suggests doing business with merchants who provide free shipping for both purchases and returns or who have a physical location nearby where they'll ship for free or accept returns.

Earn Cash Back When You Shop Online

- To lower the cost of holiday spending, you can receive cash back on purchases.

Members can get cash back from tens of thousands of online stores by using websites like BeFrugal and Ebates.

Bring your smartphone and check RetailMeNot before you buy, advised Cary Carbonaro, author of "The Money Queen's Guide: For Women Who Want to Build Wealth and Banish Fear."

Look for coupon codes

- Visit websites like Offers.com to obtain coupon codes that can be used at checkout before making any online purchases.

You can subscribe to receive email-based coupon coupons and follow your favorite retailers on Facebook and Twitter.

While you shop, use a smartphone app like Coupon Sherpa to check for deals and coupons at local brick-

and-mortar stores. If you discover a coupon you can use, scan the barcode at the register to receive a discount.

Make Use of the Online Chat Service

- You need to be a little more proactive with some holiday shopping advice.

Use the live chat functions on retailer websites this Christmas season. Inquire about special offers or even possible unpublicized reductions. You can even indicate that you're investigating a product from a rival to entice a one-time discount.

Inquire about discounts and whether they'll respect an expired coupon or recently reduced price by picking up the phone and calling customer care. Other times, all it takes is a simple discount request.

Teri Gault, the author of "Shop Smart, Save More," remarked, "Wherever I go shopping, I always ask for a discount, and I generally get it."

Chapter 4

Take Advantage of Price Matching

- Price matching is a terrific method to get the best deals without having to visit many stores, but it does take some initiative, according to Howard Schaffer of Offers.com.

You, as a consumer, are responsible for keeping an eye on product costs and providing shops with evidence that rivals are selling the same item for less. Apps like RedLaser and ShopSavvy can be useful.

You should also be aware that certain retailers have greater price-matching practices than others, according to Schaffer. Major shops like Target and Walmart have some of the finest policies, matching both the pricing of their regional rivals and those of internet merchants like Amazon.

Choose "Download Browser Tools"

- You can download free browser extensions to help you compare prices and look for deals.

As an illustration, the browser add-on Honey locates discount codes and automatically uses them while customers are checking out. This technology also finds discounts on Amazon and informs customers which vendor is providing the greatest bargain.

Watch Price Drops

- Even if you purchase products outright, you might be able to save money if they go on sale.

Many merchants, including Macy's, Sears, Target, and Walmart, give price adjustments if an item you purchase at full price is marked down within a predetermined period of time after the date of purchase.

Please 'Clear Your Cookies'

- Deals can be found in abundance online. But first, empty your cookie jar.

Websites produce cookies, which are then saved on your computer. They make websites load more quickly but can also be used to track your online activity.

According to Woroch, you should delete the cookies on your browser to prevent retailers from tracking your purchases and surfing habits, which they might use to change the pricing you see on their websites.

Use the Correct Credit Card

- Utilizing credit cards over the holidays can be advantageous if you have a routine of paying off the balance on your cards each month.

You can save money and gain points on purchases by carefully selecting and utilizing credit cards, Schaffer said. You can also more easily keep track of your spending.

Chapter 5

Redeem points for holiday money.

- Your credit card rewards could be a source of untapped money for the holidays.

To help with some of your holiday expenditures, take advantage of the opportunity to exchange your points for cash or gift cards.

Don't shop when intoxicated.

- While the holidays are a time for cheer and celebration, a little bit of drinking prior to going shopping can blow your gift budget.

Author and relationship expert April Masini stated, "Shopping while intoxicated won't get you murdered, but it will lead you to buy things you can't afford because you'll be carried away by a wave of martini-fueled happiness. Shopping and Starbucks, yep. No, you can't drink and shop."

Shopping With Cash

- Shopping with only enough money to purchase the goods on your list is an effective approach to reduce your holiday expenditures.

For someone who already has credit card debt and doesn't want to accrue more, this strategy is great. According to Woroch, using cash when you shop will not only help you avoid impulsive purchases but also halt the practice of purchasing presents for oneself.

Register for Store Rewards Programs

- Join rewards programs with stores you plan to visit during the holiday season to save money, said Schaffer.

For instance, if you sign up for Kohl's Yes2You Rewards, you will receive a $5 incentive for every 100 points you earn and receive one point for every dollar spent. A lot of retailers with loyalty programs will give members coupons, and some will raise the incentives during the Christmas sales.

Purchase at garage sales

- Financial expert Catherine Alford claimed that by purchasing gifts for her children from garage sales and on Craigslist, she is able to save money.

On Christmas morning, "all youngsters want is to have fun and play with toys," she said. They don't care how much money you spent on them or who played with the toys before them. For instance, she purchased a gently used train table with tracks and trains for less than half the original cost. You should never purchase certain products brand new.

Chapter 6

Put Your Warehouse Club Membership to Use

- You can save money over the holidays if you are a warehouse club member like Costco or Sam's Club. For instance, gift cards for well-known stores are discounted at Costco.

Furthermore, you can buy wine in bulk for holiday events.

Don't Pass Up the Dollar Store

- Look no further than your neighborhood dollar store for advice on how to save money during the holidays.

By buying specific seasonal products from clearance stores, you can save a lot of money. A roll of gift wrap or a gift bag can be purchased for just one dollar, as opposed to costing several dollars. For just one dollar, you may also get paper plates, napkins, candles, stocking stuffers, and Christmas cards. A great place to get remarkably affordable shelf-stable food items is the dollar shop.

Avoid waiting until the last minute.

- Shopping for the holidays at the last minute might be a big mistake.

Barry Choi, a personal finance expert at Money We Have, warned that waiting until December can result in you not finding what you're searching for and spending more on an alternative gift.

Choose inexpensive presents.

- Giving a thoughtful present doesn't have to cost a lot of money.

Giving magazine subscriptions was advised by Susan Kessler of The Frugal Diva. Every month, they think about how considerate you are, she added. And on Amazon, you can get yearly memberships to a range of periodicals for just $5.

It is also possible to separate a Christmas present package containing a variety of goods into gifts for employees and neighbors. Woroch suggested getting a big box of chocolates from a warehouse club and splitting them up into cellophane bags with ribbon embellishments. Even better, you can make your own jams.

Pay attention to Meaningful Gifts.

- Campbell suggested that you show your loved ones your affection and love by spending time with them rather than spending money on gifts.

She continued by saying that this might mean anything, including spending time with close friends and family, watching kids, or volunteering an hour of your time to use your abilities to help others.

Chapter 7

Make Your Own Ornaments is a phrase.

- You may cut costs on Christmas tree ornaments by making your own.

Woroch claims that by getting a range of inexpensive things from craft stores and even arranging a party with friends, you can make it enjoyable. If you have kids, start a Christmas ritual with them.

Save money on dining out.

- You could find yourself purchasing more meals on the fly or eating out with friends over the busy Christmas season.

You may manage the cost of dining out by buying inexpensive restaurant gift cards from Restaurant.com. For cheap restaurant gift cards, visit Gift Card Granny.

Holiday potlucks are being held.

- Instead of providing all the food for the holiday events you are hosting, ask friends and family to bring their favorite dishes, desserts, or beverages to share.

This can help you save money while also reducing your anxiety during the occasion. The best approach to feed Christmas visitors on a budget is to host a potluck.

Invest in LED bulbs.

- Lighting consumes a significant amount of electricity, and Alex Goldstein from Eligo Energy claims that LED lights are up to 10 times more efficient and last up to 50 times longer than incandescent bulbs.

Even though they might be the centerpiece of your Christmas décor, don't allow ornamental lights break your monthly spending plan. Spend money on LED bulbs so they can last for many years.

Save money by making a gift request.

- If you anticipate receiving gifts from others this holiday season, think about requesting products that will allow you to save money in the long run.

Goldstein suggested adding a self-programming Nest Thermostat and a controlled sprinkler system to lower your yearly water expenditures. Buying a straightforward gas gift card will help you save money. Anything that will enable you to reduce your energy costs, regardless of how modest, makes a terrific gift.

Making a Volunteering Gift.

- According to Steve Repak, author of "6 Week Money Challenge," you might spend less money on gifts and more time volunteering during the holidays.

Repak suggested asking friends and family to give some of their time at a soup kitchen, homeless shelter, or charity in lieu of giving each other gifts.

Everyone can do this to get in the holiday spirit, but kids and teenagers in particular, he said.

Create a "No-Gift Christmas".

- Christenson remembered trying to arrange a Christmas without presents for his family.

Added he, "I suggested we do something as a family, like go to a nice restaurant, see a movie, or celebrate a particular occasion, instead of giving gifts. You could even establish a new, enduring family tradition.

Think about having a Christmas party after Christmas.

However, delaying your trip until January will help you avoid a ton of hassle, stress, and expense "said Greg Geronemus, a recognized travel expert and co-CEO of smarTours. At the airports and train stations, there will be a great deal less trouble and chaos, as well as far better and cheaper prices and a great deal less stress.

You could also decide to postpone gift-giving and take advantage of deals by waiting until after Christmas.

Summary

The National Retail Federation predicted that retail sales will increase by 3.6% to 4% in November and December. Two-thirds of Americans want to spend at least $100 more on holiday shopping this year than usual. Here are 40 strategies for reducing holiday expenditures and relieving financial stress. Spreading out your purchases will allow you to budget well *and prevent a credit hangover in January. Establishing a defined budget for their gifts can help your children create a gift wishlist rather than letting them swoon over every new toy and gadget that's released this holiday season.*

Amazon, Best Buy, Target and Walmart may be offering early Black Friday bargains. Staying up late the night before Thanksgiving will pay off handsomely. Black Friday is a popular time for people to buy things and then resell them online. Your home is full of hidden revenue opportunities that will materialize during the holiday season. Even leftover ink cartridges can be turned into holiday cash.

Use pre-owned and refurbished electronics to save money this holiday season. Earn Cash Back When You Shop Online to help lower the cost of holiday spending. Use Discounted Gift Cards from websites like CardCash and Giftcard Zen. If you purchase products outright, you might be able to save money if they go on sale. Delete cookies from your browser to prevent retailers from tracking your purchases and surfing habits.

Shopping while intoxicated can lead you to buy things you can't afford because of a wave of happiness. Join rewards programs with stores you plan to visit during the holiday season to save money. A great place to get remarkably affordable shelf-stable food items is the dollar store. You may cut costs on Christmas tree ornaments by making your own. It is possible to separate a Christmas present package containing a variety of goods into gifts for employees and neighbors.

You could find yourself purchasing more meals on the fly or eating out with friends over the busy Christmas season. If you anticipate receiving gifts this holiday season, think about requesting products that will allow you to save money in the long run. Steve Repak suggests asking friends and family to give some of their time at a soup kitchen, homeless shelter or charity in lieu of giving each other gifts.

Printed in Great Britain
by Amazon

19922026R00031